General Editor: Aidan Chambers

DRAGON SLAYER

This is the story of Beowulf, the legendary fighter, a man
with the strength of thirty men in his arms. He it was
who rid the Danes of a deadly scourge: the prowling
monster who struck terror into the bravest hearts. He it
was who fought Grendel and his fearful mother, and the
dragon who guarded the treasure-hoard hidden in the
earth.

Rosemary Sutcliff was born in Surrey, and has often been
honoured as a writer of stories drawn from history and
legend. She has written a great many books among which
are: *The Eagle of the Ninth* (Oxford University Press),
Warrior Scarlet (Oxford University Press), *Sun Horse, Moon
Horse* (Bodley Head).

DRAGON SLAYER

The Story of Beowulf

Rosemary Sutcliff

Illustrated by Charles Keeping

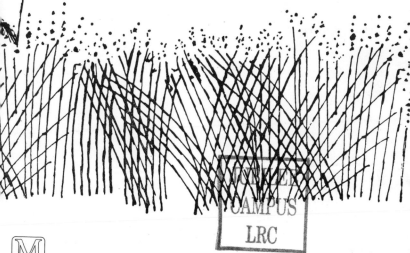

BOOKS

Macmillan Education

© Rosemary Sutcliff 1961
Illustrations © The Bodley Head Ltd 1961

First published in Great Britain as *Beowulf*
by The Bodley Head 1961

First published in *M Books* 1980

Published by
MACMILLAN EDUCATION LIMITED
Houndmills Basingstoke Hampshire RG21 2XS
and London
Associated companies in Delhi Dublin
Hong Kong Johannesburg Lagos Melbourne
New York Singapore and Tokyo

Printed in Hong Kong

Contents

1. The Seafarers, 7
2. The Danish Shore, 17
3. Hrothgar's Hall, 27
4. Grendel, 39
5. Terror Comes Again, 53
6. The Sea-Hag, 65
7. The Sail-Road Home, 75
8. The Fire-Drake's Hoard, 83
9. The Death of Beowulf, 95

1. The Seafarers

In the great hall of Hygelac, King of the Geats, supper was over and the mead horns going round. It was the time of evening, with the dusk gathering beyond the firelight, when the warriors called for Angelm the King's bard to wake his harp for their amusement; but tonight they had something else to listen to than the half-sung, half-told stories of ancient heroes that they knew by heart. Tonight there were strangers in their midst, seafarers with the salt still in their hair, from the first trading ship to reach them since the ice melted and the wild geese came North again. And their Captain sat in the Guest Seat that faced the High Seat of the King, midway up the hall, and told the news of the coasts and islands and the northern seas.

He leaned forward in the great carved seat, a small man with his hands on his knees, and his long-sighted seaman's gaze coming and going about the smoky hall, and told, among lesser matters, how Hrothgar, the great warrior king of the Danish folk, had built for himself a mighty mead-hall where he and his household

8

warriors might feast and make merry, and give a fitting welcome to any strangers and wayfarers who came among them.

'A great hall, a most fine hall!' said the Sea Captain, while the rest of his crew on the mead benches nodded and muttered their agreement. 'Longer and loftier even than this in which my lord Hygelac has feasted us so royally tonight. And Hrothgar set up high on its gable end the gilded antlers of a stag, and called the place for that reason, Heorot the Hart. Aye, but he might have done better to have lived out his days in a shepherd's bothie; for small joy has the Danish King of his mead-hall.' And he drank deep from the mead horn as it was handed to him, and shook his head, and waited to be asked why.

Hygelac laughed a little, playing with the ears of Heardred his small son, as though the boy had been a favourite hound propped against his knee. 'And why has the Danish King such small joy of his mead-hall?'

'Because,' said the Sea Captain, 'before even a King makes merry, it is as well that he should know who may hear the laughter in the dark outside.' And eager as he was to tell the story, he glanced aside into the blue dusk that thickened beyond the foreporch doorway.

'Who heard?' demanded Hygelac, no longer

laughing; and the sea beyond the keel-strand sounded very near as they waited.

The Sea Captain looked about him as though gathering his hearers closer; he would have made a story-teller to equal Angelm, if he had chosen the harp instead of the steering-oar. 'Grendel, the Night Stalker,' he said at last. 'Grendel the Man-Wolf, the Death-Shadow, who has his lair among the sea inlets and the coastal marshes. He heard the laughter and the harp-song from the King's high hall, and it troubled him in his dark dreams, and he roused and came up out of the waste lands and snuffed about the porch. The door stood unfastened in the usual way – though it would have been little hindrance to *him* had it been barred to keep out a war-host.' His listeners nodded, and huddled

closer to the long fires, and here and there a man glanced behind him into the shadows. They all knew that bolts and bars could no more keep out the Trollkind than blade of mortal forging could bite on their scaly hides.

'Grendel prowled in, hating all men and all joy, and hungry for human life. So swift was his attack that no man heard an outcry; but when the dawn came, thirty of Hrothgar's best and noblest thanes were missing, and only the blood splashed on walls and floors, and the monster's footprints oozing red, remained to tell their fate.'

A deep murmur ran from man to man all up and down the crowded hall, and Hygelac said, 'This is an evil story that you tell, my friend.'

'Aye, evil enough, and the end is not yet reached, for having once roused, the Night

Stalker does not sleep again, but comes back and back and back; and to this day after the dark comes down Heorot is a place forsaken and accursed.'

'But can Hrothgar find no champions in all Denmark strong enough to rid him of this horror?'

The Sea Captain shook his head. 'At first there were plenty bold enough to spend the night in Hrothgar's hall – especially when the mead was in them. But in the morning nothing was ever left of them save the blood splashed on the floor. And so the time came long since when no more champions could be found.'

'And still he comes, this monster, even though the hall is empty?'

'Perhaps he hopes always for the time when some man sleeps again in Heorot the Hart. Still he comes; and every morning the miry foot-prints and the salt-marsh smell are left to tell where Grendel prowled among the mead benches in the last night's dark. And Hrothgar the King grows old in sorrow, and in hope; but he can have little hope left him now – that one day Wyrd who weaves the fates of men may send him a champion strong enough to free him and his people from the Death-Shadow that fills their nights with horror.'

Among the thanes crowding the long benches,

one leaned forward, his arms across his knees
and his eyes levelled on the Sea Captain's face,
as though the dark tale struck closer home to
him than to the rest. A young man, fair-headed
and grey-eyed as most of his fellows were, but
taller than they by half a head, and with strength
that could out-wrestle the great Northern bear
showing in the quiet muscles of his neck and
shoulders. He sat in a place that was not particularly high, nor yet particularly lowly; indeed,
he was one who seldom cared about his rightful
place unless another man thought to deny it to
him. Yet there was something in his face and his
whole bearing that would have marked him for
what he was, even to the passing glance of a
stranger. For this was Beowulf, sister's-son to
the King and foremost among his warriors.

To the other men in Hygelac's hall that night
the seafarer's story had been no more than a
far-off tale, though one to raise the neck-hair
and set one glancing into the shadows; but to
Beowulf it was word of a friend in dire trouble,
and an old debt waiting to be paid.

Long since, before Beowulf was born, Ecgtheow his father had killed one of the powerful
tribe of the Wylfings; and, like many another
man who had become embroiled in a blood feud,
he had taken to the wild life of a sea-rover,
carrying off his young wife to share it with him.

Storm-driven, they had come to the Court of Hrothgar, and there, through the years that followed, the young rover had found such a friend in the Danish King as few men find in their need. Ecgtheow was dead now, but his son, born at the Danish Court, had not forgotten. Besides, he himself knew well the life of a sea-rover, and the longing for adventure that was in his blood had been stirring in him these past weeks, as it did every year when the thaw came and the birch buds thickened. He thought of his long war-boat, freshly caulked and painted after the storms of last year, waiting for him in the boat shed as a mare waits for her rider; and he took his gaze from the Sea Captain's face and glanced about him at the faces of his companions, his shoulder-to-shoulder men who had taken the seaways with him in other summers.

And out of the shadows and the firelight and the flare of the torches, Waegmund his kinsman and young Hondscio and Scaef and the rest looked back at him with brightening eyes, once more a brotherhood and a war-boat's crew.

Then Beowulf got to his feet, and strode up the hall to stand before the High Seat where Hygelac sat with his small son against his knee. 'My lord Hygelac, I ask your leave to go on a seafaring.'

Hygelac looked at his young kinsman keenly.

'Maybe I will give you leave to follow the sea-roads again; but first tell me what is in your heart.'

'When my father needed a friend at his shoulder, he found such a one in this Hrothgar of the Danes,' Beowulf said. 'Shelter he gave to my father and my mother, and to me also when the time came that she bore me; and my first memories are of lying on a wolfskin before his fire. He paid the Wergild, the fine for the man my father slew, and made peace between him and the Wylfings, so that a time came in my sixth summer when my father might return home to his own kind again. Now it seems that Hrothgar himself stands sorely in need of a friend and it is time for me to repay the debt.'

Hygelac bent his head, and trouble lay like a shadow on his face. 'I thought so. I thought so ... Beowulf, sister's-son, you are foremost among my warriors, and save for the boy here, you are almost the only kinsman left to me; and I grieve to see you go upon such a perilous seafaring. Yet a man should pay his debts. Go then, but remember that there will be anxious eyes watching here from the clifftops for your returning sail at sea.'

2. The Danish Shore

Hrothgar's Coast Warden, sitting his horse on the clifftop northward of Heorot, saw a strange vessel running in from the open sea, between the high headlands at the mouth of the fjord. A war-galley, long and slim and swift; and the light blinked on the painted shields hung along her bulwarks and the grey battlegear of the men who swung to her oars. Her square striped sail fell slack as the headland took the wind from it, and then came rattling down, and urged by her rowers she headed like some eager many-legged sea creature for the low shelving beach where the cliffs dropped at the head of the fjord.

Frowning, the Coast Warden wheeled his horse, and touching his heel to its flank, urged it into the cliff path that looped down in the same direction. He came out through the furze and the salt-burned bush-tangle above the shore, just as the strange war-boat came lightly in through the shallows. Her crew unshipped their oars and sprang overboard into the white oar-thresh while it still foamed along her sides, and

18

now they were running her up the shingle to strand on the tideline.

Fifteen of them, the Coast Warden counted; and the sunlight sparkled on their weapons as

they swung their painted linden shields clear of the bulwarks; and yet they had not the wolf-pack look of a raiding band. Again he touched his heel to his horse's flank and, spear in hand, rode down into their midst, where they turned at the sound of hooves and stood waiting for his coming, gathered about the upreared dragon prow of their vessel.

To one who was clearly the leader among them, a very tall man whose eyes were coloured like deep water on a cloudy day, the Coast Warden spoke boldly, yet courteously enough. 'Who are you, strangers from across the sea, and what purpose brings you to this landfall on the Danish shore? You come in war array, armed as for battle, yet you have not the look of those who come to burn farms and drive off women and cattle.'

'In truth, though we come in war array, the battle that we seek is not with the Danish folk,' the tall man said. 'As to who we are – I am Beowulf, sister's-son to Hygelac King of the Geats, and these with me are my sword-brothers and hearth-companions. As to our purpose – a few days since, word came to Hygelac's Court that Hrothgar of the Danes was in need of champions to rid him of the monster that walks his hall at night; and so we are come, following the Whale's Road southward across the grey Baltic from our own strand.'

For a long moment, while the surf creamed on the shore, the Coast Warden sat his horse and looked at them, his eyes narrowed under his brows; he was old and a judge of men. Then he nodded. 'So. It is long and long that Hrothgar and all his folk have waited for such champions. Come then, and I will set you on your way to the King's hall.'

'First we must make all secure here,' said Beowulf, and he reached up his hand and set it on the swell of the painted dragon-prow above him, caressingly as though it were a living thing. 'Horse or vessel should be tended first of all things at a journey's end.'

'Have no fear for your proud vessel. I will send trustworthy men of my own to make all fast with a barricade of oars against the high tide.' The old man was eager now. 'If you are indeed the champions you seem, let Hrothgar my lord wait no longer, for he has waited over long already for help,' and he pointed along a rough track that wound up from the beach through the furze and the hazel thickets. 'See, our way lies yonder.'

In single file, for the track was too narrow to walk abreast, Beowulf and his comrades followed the old Warden on his horse up from the head of the fjord, a grey mailed serpent of men, the forged rings of their battle-sarks ringing as they moved. On the crest of the ridge where the wind-shaped trees fell back, the track changed abruptly into a paved road, and there they checked, with the sea wind humming against their mailed shoulders. Behind them was the way home, the fjord running out between its nesses to the open sea, and the war-boat lying like a basking seal among the brown sea-wrack and the drift-wood on the high tide line. Ahead of them lay the unknown and the hazard that they had come to seek. From their feet the land dropped away into a shallow vale, then rose again to sombre moors inland, and a mile off, in the trough of the vale between the coast and the moors, Beowulf, narrowing his eyes into the sunlight, could see a great hall rising among a scatter of lesser roofs, the green and brown of tilled land, the darker dapple of orchard trees. And straight towards the hall, purposeful as the

flight of an arrow, ran the paved road on which he stood.

'Yonder is Heorot,' said the Coast Warden's voice in his ear. 'The road will take you to the very doorsill. I must be away back to the coast, but do you go forward now, my friends, and have no fear for your ship; she shall be well tended.' And without another word he swung his horse in a half circle and was gone, trampling away down the rough track behind them. And Beowulf and his companions went forward alone.

Down from the high coast-wise ridge they strode, into the green pasture lands where the cattle and horses grazed, through the cornland

where the young barley was already a mist of green over the dark earth, between the first heather-thatched homesteads of the settlement, each with its bee skeps along the wall and its few apple trees, where children and dogs and lean pigs were playing together, and women grinding corn or spinning in their doorways looked up to watch the strangers pass.

It all seemed peaceful enough – now, with the sun still high in the sky.

In the midst of the settlement the roof of the King's hall rose higher and higher as they drew towards it; Heorot the Hart, heather-thatched like all the rest, but with the gilded antlers on the gable ends proudly uptossed towards the sky. Straight to the foreporch doorway ran the paved road; and up it, their war-gear sounding on them as the feathers of wild swans sound in flight, strode the fifteen Geats.

In the doorway one of the household thanes stood leaning on a spear; a dark man with beads of yellow sea-washed amber round his neck. His gaze was upon them as they came to a halt before him; and he asked, as the Coast Warden had asked, 'Who are you, strangers who come in war-harness to the threshold of Hrothgar the King? And what is it that you seek here?'

'As to who we are – I am sister's-son to Hygelac, King of the Geats, and these with me

are my sword-brothers and hearth-companions,'
Beowulf replied, as he had done before. 'As to
what we seek here – we would have word with
Hrothgar the King, for our business is with
him.'

'Wait then, and I will carry your name to
Hrothgar,' said the man, and turned back into
the fire-flickered shadows behind him, from
which came men's voices and the smell of roast
meat.

Beowulf and his comrades sat down on the
guest-bench in the sunlight before the door, but
they had only a short time to wait before the
door-thane returned, and at his bidding they
stacked their shields and ashen spears against
the wall, and followed him into the hall where
Hrothgar's house-thanes sat at meat.

Great and splendid indeed was Heorot to the
gaze of Beowulf as he stepped across the door
sill on to the many-coloured flagstones of the
floor. Down the midst of the hall the fires blazed
on their three hearths, and the smoke curled up-
wards to find its way out through the openings
in the roof high overhead, and through the
drifting haze that hung about the place he saw
the warriors at the long tables, with mead horns
and boar flesh and huge piles of barley cakes
before them; saw too the walls and roof-trees
rich with worked hangings and ornaments of

white walrus ivory, and the shields and spears of the warriors hung above the mead benches.

Hrothgar's High Seat was not midway up the hall, as was the High Seat in Hygelac's hall, but on a raised dais at the far end, and so the Geatish warriors must walk the full length of the place, between the long trestle tables, to come to him; and all tongues fell silent and every eye was turned upon them, but especially upon their tall leader, as they passed.

At the step of the dais Beowulf halted and stood proudly confronting Hrothgar; and the Danish King leaned forward, hands clenched on the foreposts of his great carved seat, to stare down at him.

3. Hrothgar's Hall

Beowulf remembered the stern yet kindly features on the very farmost fringes of his memory. But Hrothgar was old now, the lines on his face were bitten deep as sword-cuts by years of grief, and the beard that jutted over the broad gold-work collar at his throat was grey as a badger's pelt.

'So it is true,' the old man said broodingly, after a long silence. 'I scarce believed ... But there is that in your face that I should know again if you stood among a hundred warriors; aye, though you stood no higher at the shoulder, when last I saw you, than Garm my favourite hound. My heart leapt up within me when Wulfnoth my door-thane brought word that Beowulf, sister's-son to the Geatish King, sat waiting on my guest-bench to have speech with me – and most joyfully are you welcome, you and your comrades with you. But tell me what brings you here to my threshold as your father came. Have you too slain a man of the Wylfings?'

Beowulf shook his head, answering the sad flash of a smile that lit for an instant the old

28

man's face. 'Na, na, my lord Hrothgar. Sea-faring men brought to Geatland word of the evil that has fallen upon the Danish King and his folk; and so we come, I and my sword-brothers, to offer our services and our strength against the thing that walks Heorot in the dark. Men say that I have the strength of thirty warriors in my grip.' He raised his arms as he spoke, and held them out to the old King in a gesture that was half proud and half pleading. 'And it is yours, for my father's sake. Give to me and my comrades leave to sleep in your hall tonight.'

Hrothgar bent his face into his hands, then he raised it again, and looked long and earnestly at Beowulf who stood tall as a spear in his grey war-gear before him. 'So you have come for friendship's sake,' he said at last, 'for the sake of the bond that was between Ecgtheow your father and myself when the world was young. Yet think before it is too late; think of the hideous end that has come to every man who has stood in this place to pit his strength and courage against the Death-Shadow-in-the-Dark. Grendel's strength cannot be measured even against the strength of thirty men, for it is beyond the measuring of mortal strength. They also were young and strong, those other champions who have stood here before you, but youth and strength did not avail them. In the name of the old friendship that brought you here I bid you think, and be very sure, before the time for thinking is past.'

'We have thought, all of us, and we are content to abide whatever the night may bring,' Beowulf said. 'The outcome must be as Wyrd who weaves the fates of men may choose.'

The light of great hope kindled slowly in the King's face, and he straightened himself in the high carved seat. 'So be it, then: I accept the aid that you bring me, Beowulf, son of Ecgtheow. Sleep in my hall tonight, but meanwhile do you and those who come with you feast with high hearts among my thanes.'

At this, a clamour of voices, fiercely joyful, arose from the warriors who had held their listening silence while Beowulf and the King spoke together; and room and welcome were made for the strangers on the crowded benches. Beowulf found himself sitting between Hrothgar's two young sons. Steaming boar's flesh and eel pie were set before him and a great mead horn thrust into his hands, and the feasting in Heorot roared up like a fire when dry birch bark is flung on to it.

But one man in all that thronged hall did not rejoice at Beowulf's coming. Hunferth the King's Speech-maker and Jester, sitting at his lord's feet, could not endure that any man should shine above himself. Bitter-tongued and envious, fierce-tempered in his cups, he waited until the noise of feasting lulled for a moment, then rose to his feet and spoke coolly and jibingly to the tall guest.

'Tell us, now, are you that Beowulf of whom we have heard, who strove with Breca son of Beanstan in a wondrous contest upon the winter sea?'

Beowulf, who had been laughing with the King's sons, looked up and saw the speaker, standing below the High Seat, the bitter face flushed with drink, the glittering eyes and mocking smile. 'So that story has come ahead of me to the Danish folk,' he said.

'Aye, it is a fine story, and we have heard it all.' Hunferth swayed a little and steadied himself. 'We have heard how your friends and kindred begged you to forbear such folly, and how you would not heed them, but pushed off into the waves of the rising storm. Seven days and nights you pitted yourselves against each other, so men say. Yet in the end it was Breca who had the mastery. And should you not have thought, before you came here like a cock crowing on another's dunghill, that Grendel is like to be a fiercer and a stronger foe than ever Breca son of Beanstan could be?'

There was a moment's hush in the long hall:

no sound save the crackle of flames on the hearths and the worrying of two hounds over a bone. Then Beowulf sprang to his feet, oversetting the mead horn and leaving it to drip unheeded on to the many-coloured pavement. He was a peaceable man, slow to wrath and swift to forget an injury; so peaceable that at first men had scorned him for it, until they learned the unwisdom of such scorn. But he could be angry, and he was angry now. 'So, you have heard the old story; but it seems that you have heard it amiss, my large-mouthed friend. Maybe your ears were too full of heather beer for clear listening! It was a folly, even as you say, a youthful folly; we were boys, Breca and I, and never foes. We boasted against each other who could slay the most walrus without once putting in to land, and having boasted, we must make good our boasts. So we took each of us a small boat, and put out into the Whale's Road. Our swords we wore naked and beside we had long walrus hooks and spears, but the swords were for our own defence in case of need, not for use against each other; and five days we held our course side by side, but could not find the walrus that we had come to seek. And then, off the coast of Finland, a great storm arose and drove our boats apart, and when dawn came I was near to shore – aye, and I had found the walrus. They were all about me in the troughs of the waves; one, the greatest of them all, made for the boat. I speared him, but missed the life-place, and in our struggle and the weltering of the seas the boat was overturned and together, locked in battle, we went down and down into the icy depths. Then I had good use for my sword, for with it I contrived at last to end the creature's life, and so rose again, my breast bursting, to the light of day. The sea beasts were all about me, they rushed upon me with their white tusks bared to gash me limb from limb. But I had still my sword, and so at last I was wave-flung upon the sea-strand of Finland, and the bodies of nine great walrus with me. Breca, as I learned after, came also to the shore, but in a place far off from mine, and *he* did not find the walrus herd. Not Breca, therefore, but *I* was the victor in that contest!'

Beowulf threw back his head like a wolfhound when it bays defiance, and the fierce laughter rang in his voice. 'I have not heard tell of any great deeds of yours, King's Jester, that give you the right to question mine! If you were a man more for doing and less for talking maybe your Hearth-Lord would have found his champion to rid him of the fiend Grendel ere this!'

A roar of laughter beat up from the crowded benches, and Hunferth's hollow face flushed more darkly than before. He made as though to hurl some other insult, but the sympathies of every man in Heorot were with the stranger, and he could only shrug his shoulders and smile as though the whole matter were a jest, and lounge down again on his stool at the King's feet.

Beowulf, quietly as though nothing had happened, settled himself once more upon the bench, righted the mead horn, and returned to his half-eaten barley cake.

So the feasting continued, and men grew fiercely merry, and the harper stood up to make music beside the King's hearth. Then the hangings of embroidered stuff that closed the doorway to the women's quarters were drawn aside, and a woman stood there with others behind her, a tall woman in a crimson robe, dark-eyed and dark-haired, with royal gold-work about her head, and in her hands a great golden cup.

She had no part with Hrothgar in Beowulf's early memory, for she was a second wife, and much younger than her lord, but looking at her, he knew that she must be Wealhtheow the Queen. She came forward, her women behind her, and the cheerful uproar lulled at her coming. She carried the golden cup first to Hrothgar, where he sat in his High Seat, saying in a clear voice that reached to the farthest end of the hall, 'We have heard, even in the women's quarters, of the champions from across the sea who feast in Heorot this evening; and we have heard the brave purpose of their coming. Surely now our sorrows are almost over; therefore drink, my dear lord, and let your heart be lightened.'

And when the King had drunk, she carried the cup from one to another of the warriors, Geat and Dane alike, all down the benches, while one of her women coming behind with the mead jar refilled for her as often as the cup grew low. Last of all she came to Beowulf where he sat as

35

guest of honour between her two sons. 'Greeting, and joy be to you, Beowulf son of Ecgtheow; and all the thanks of our hearts, that you come so valiantly to our aid.'

Beowulf rose to his feet and took the cup as she held it out to him. 'Valour is a word to use when the battle is over,' he said, smiling. 'Give us your thanks, great Queen, when we have done the thing which we come to do. But this at least I promise you, that if we fail to rid you of the monster, we shall not live to carry home our shields.' And throwing back his head, he drained the cup and gave it again into her hands.

But now the shadows were gathering in the corners of the hall, and as the daylight faded, a shadow seemed to gather on the hearts of all men there, a shadow that was all too long familiar to the Danes. Then Hrothgar rose in his High Seat, and called Beowulf to him again.

'Soon it will be dusk,' he said, when the young Geat stood before him. 'And yet again the time of dread comes upon Heorot. You are still determined upon this desperate venture?'

'I am not wont to change my purpose without cause,' Beowulf said, 'and those with me are of a like mind, or they would not have taken ship with me from Geatland in the first place.'

'So. Keep watch, then. If you prevail in the combat before you, you shall have such reward from me as never yet heroes had from a King. I pray to the All-Father that when the light grows again out of tonight's dark, you may stand here to claim it. Heorot is yours until morning.' And he turned and walked out through the postern door, a tall old man stooping under the burden of his own height, to his sleeping quarters, where Wealhtheow the Queen had gone before him.

All up and down the hall men were taking leave of each other, dwindling away to their own sleeping places for the night. The thralls set back the benches and stacked the trestle boards against the gable-walls, and spread out straw-filled bolsters and warm wolfskin rugs for the fifteen warriors. Then they too were gone, and Heorot was left to the band of Geats, and the dreadful thing whose shadow was already creeping towards them through the dark.

'Bar the doors,' Beowulf said, when the last footsteps of the last thrall had died away. 'Bars will not keep him out, but at least they may give us some warning of his coming.'

And when two of them had done his bidding, and the seldom-used bars were in their sockets, there was nothing more that could be done.

For a little, as the last fire sank lower, they stood about it, sometimes looking at each other, sometimes into the glowing embers, seldom speaking. Not one of them had much hope that he would see the daylight again, yet none repented of having followed their leader upon the venture. One by one, the fourteen lay down in their harness, with their swords beside them. But Beowulf stripped off his battle-sark and gave it with his sword and boar-crested helmet to Waegmund his kinsman and the dearest to him of all his companions, for he knew that mortal weapons were of no use against the Troll-kind; such creatures must be mastered, if they could be mastered at all, by a man's naked strength, and the red courage of his heart.

Then he too lay down, as though to sleep.

4. Grendel

In the darkest hour of the spring night Grendel came to Heorot as he had come so many times before, up from his lair and over the high moors, through the mists that seemed to travel with him under the pale moon; Grendel, the Night-Stalker, the Death-Shadow. He came to the foreporch and snuffed about it, and smelled the man-smell, and found that the door which had stood unlatched for him so long was barred and bolted. Snarling in rage that any man should dare attempt to keep him out, he set the flat of his talon-tipped hands against the timbers and burst them in.

Dark as it was, the hall seemed to fill with a monstrous shadow at his coming; a shadow in which Beowulf, half springing up, then holding himself in frozen stillness, could make out no shape nor clear outline save two eyes filled with a wavering greenish flame.

The ghastly corpse-light of his own eyes showed Grendel the shapes of men as it seemed sleeping, and he did not notice among them one who leaned up on his elbow. Laughing in his throat, he reached out and grabbed young Hondscio who lay nearest to him, and almost before his victim had time to cry out, tore him limb from limb and drank the warm blood. Then, while the young warrior's dying shriek still hung upon the air, he reached for another. But this time his hand was met and seized in a grasp such as he had never felt before; a grasp that had in it the strength of thirty men. And for the first time he who had brought fear to so many caught the taste of it himself, knowing that at last he had met his match and maybe his master.

Beowulf leapt from the sleeping bench and grappled him in the darkness; and terror broke over Grendel in full force, the terror of a wild animal trapped; so that he thought no more of his hunting but only of breaking the terrible hold upon his arm and flying back into the night and the wilderness, and he howled and bellowed as he struggled for his freedom. Beowulf set his teeth and summoned all his strength and tightened his grip until the sinews cracked; and locked together they reeled and staggered up and down the great hall. Trestles and sleeping benches went over with crash on crash as they strained this way and that, trampling even through the last red embers of the dying fire; and the very walls seemed to groan and shudder

as though the stout timbers would burst apart.
And all the while Grendel snarled and shrieked
and Beowulf fought in silence save for his
gasping breaths.

Outside, the Danes listened in horror to the
turmoil that seemed as though it must split
Heorot asunder; and within, the Geats had
sprung from their sleeping benches sword in
hand, forgetful of their powerlessness against
the Troll-kind, but in the dark, lit only by stray
gleams of bale-fire from the monster's eyes, they
dared not strike for fear of slaying their leader,
and when one or other of them did contrive to
get in a blow, the sword blade glanced off
Grendel's charmed hide as though he were
sheathed in dragon scales.

At last, when the hall was wrecked to the walls,
the Night-Stalker gathered himself for one last
despairing effort to break free. Beowulf's hold
was as fierce as ever; yet none the less the two
figures burst apart – and Grendel with a frightful
shriek staggered to the doorway and through it,
and fled wailing into the night, leaving his arm
and shoulder torn from the roots in the hero's
still unbroken grasp.

Beowulf sank down sobbing for breath on a
shattered bench, and his fellows came crowding
round him with torches rekindled at the scattered
embers of the fire; and together they looked at

the thing he held across his knees. 'Not even the Troll-kind could live half a day with a wound such as that upon them,' one of them said; and Waegmund agreed. 'He is surely dead as though he lay here among the benches.'

'Hondscio is avenged, at all events,' said Beowulf. 'Let us hang up this thing for a trophy, and a proof that we do not boast idly as the wind blows over.'

So in triumph they nailed up the huge scaly arm on one of the roof beams above the High Seat of Hrothgar.

The first thin light of day was already washing over the moors, and almost before the grizzly thing was securely in place the Danes returned to Heorot. They came thronging in to beat Beowulf in joyful acclaim upon his bruised and claw-marked shoulders, and gaze up in awe at the huge arm whose taloned fingers seemed even now to be striving to claw down the roof beam. Many of them called for their horses and followed the blood trail that Grendel had left in his flight up through the tilled land and over the moors until they came to the deep sea-inlet where the monster had his lair, and saw the churning waves between the rocks all fouled and boiling with blood. Meanwhile others set all things on foot for a day of rejoicing, and the young men wrestled together and raced their

horses against each other, filling the day with their merrymaking, while the King's harper walked to and fro by himself under the apple trees, making a song in praise of Beowulf ready for the evening's feasting which this night would not end when darkness fell.

At last Hrothgar and his Queen came from their own place, with his chief thanes and her women behind them, to hear the story of the night's battle and gaze up at the bloody trophy nailed to the roof beam.

'I hoped to force the Night-Prowler down on to one of the sleeping benches and there choke the foul life out of him,' Beowulf said, rubbing his shoulders. 'In that I failed, for despite all my strength he broke free of Heorot after all. Yet as you see, he left his arm with me as ransom for the rest of his carcass; and it is in my mind that not even Grendel may long outlive such a wound as he carries with him.'

Hrothgar gazed long and silently at the arm, then brought his gaze down to the face of the young warrior, and his eyes were bright as they had not been for many a long day. 'So it is in my mind also,' he said. 'Much sorrow have we suffered at Grendel's hands, my folk and I; many staunch warriors I have wept for in the years since Heorot was built – this hall that should have been our joy.'

'But the sorrow is passed, and now it shall be your joy indeed,' Beowulf said.

'Aye, now it shall be our joy indeed ... And that is your doing. Well might Ecgtheow your father rejoice in Valhalla in the fame that you have won; well may your mother if she yet lives praise the All-Father for the son she bore – the son she bore at my court, to be a friend and champion to me in my old age.' Hrothgar laid his arm across Beowulf's great shoulders and was near to weeping. 'From this day forward you shall be a son to me in love, and there is nothing that I would give to my own sons that you may not have from me for the asking.'

The hall was cleaned of all signs of the struggle that had raged there in the night, fresh fern was strewn about the hearths, benches and trestle boards brought in to replace those that had been broken, and the walls were hung with new embroideries from the chests in the women's quarters, on which the cunning wormknots and the serpent-tailed birds glimmered with gold in the light of the rekindled fires. And hasty preparations were made for a feast such as had never been known in Heorot before, even on the first night of all. Hrothgar made Beowulf sit beside him in the High Seat, and all down the hall Danes and Geats sat side by side, drinking deep to Beowulf the Hero from the great mead horns, and making loudly merry, only falling silent to listen while the harper sang the triumph song that he had made under the apple trees earlier that day.

When the feasting was at its height Hrothgar called to certain of his thanes. 'Now the time has come for gift making. Go now, my friends, and bring in those gifts that I have made ready for the Geatish champions who have so nobly earned them.'

And the men went out, and returned bowed under the weight of the precious things they bore, and set them down in a gleaming pile before the King.

Then the King gave to Beowulf a magnificent gold-embroidered banner, and a helmet and a battle-sark and a drinking cup all curiously worked with gold, and a great heavy sword wrought by the dwarf-kind long ago in the dark caverns beneath the earth. Then eight splendid horses were led into the hall and brought to the Geatish leader to touch their proud crests in token of acceptance; and on the foam-white back of the finest of them was strapped Hrothgar's own war saddle, gold-sheathed and rich with red coral and yellow Baltic amber. For each of Beowulf's companions also there was a sword as fine as their leader's. 'Fourteen swords,' said Hrothgar, as he gave the last into the last warrior's hand. 'Sorely I grieve that there is no fifteenth. But a sword is of little worth to a dead man; and so for Hondscio who died last night – this.' And he held out to Beowulf a bag of gold arm-rings that had been weighed out earlier that day. 'The Wergild for a brave man – for his kinsfolk who wait for him in Geatland, where he will not come again.'

'The day that we land on our own shore, before evening of that day, shall the gold and the King's words be with Hondscio's kindred,' Beowulf said. But though the young warrior was avenged, his heart was sore as he laid the gold with his own gifts, that he must go home with one lacking from the brotherhood.

While the horses still trampled and tossed their heads and snorted at the firelight, the curtains over the bower doorway parted as they had done last evening, and Wealhtheow the Queen came through them in her crimson robe, walking tall under the royal gold-work on her head, and her women following behind her.

She carried the mead cup to the King her lord, as she had done before, and held it for him to drink. 'You have made your gifts to this new son that you have taken to your heart,' she said, smiling. 'And now it is my turn, and I have brought gifts of my own from the women's quarters.' And she turned to Beowulf and held out the cup to him also. 'For the thing that you have done for us, may you live valiant and beloved to the end of your days. My sons are your brothers now; be a friend and a brother to them in their need, for they could find none better in all the world.'

Then from the women who followed her she took two gold arm-rings each fit for an earl, and a sark of link-mail so fine that it hung from her hands in folds like silk and glimmered living silver as a salmon's skin, and lastly a jewelled collar of ancient workmanship such as Beowulf had never seen or even dreamed of before; and each of these things she gave to the Geatish leader. 'Beowulf, if ever you find yourself forgetting us, wear this to help your memory,' she said as she placed the collar about his throat.

Beowulf smiled. 'I shall not need even so fair a jewel as this to aid my memory of the friends I have found at Hrothgar's Court.'

'That is well,' said the Queen, 'for I think that your friends at Hrothgar's Court will long remember you.' Then gathering her women about her she went out, quietly and proudly as she had come, between the heavy curtains into the women's quarters.

Long and long the feasting continued, and Hrothgar himself took the harp from his bard and sang the stories that the warriors had used to sing round the fires in the long winter nights when he was young. Outside, it had grown dark long since, but the revellers no longer feared the shadows, and kept the fires up and passed the harp and the mead horns from hand to hand until at last their eyes grew heavy and the time was come for sleeping. Then Hrothgar rose, and bidding his thanes a good night, withdrew to his own place, where Wealhtheow the Queen waited for him; and Beowulf and his sword-brothers were borne off to the guest-place that had been made ready in their honour. And in Heorot the Hart, the King's house-thanes lay down to sleep in their proper places, each man with his weapons and his round linden shield hanging on the wall above his head.

5. Terror Comes Again

But the time when men might sleep safely in the King's hall was not yet come. Grendel had fled away over the moors with the life streaming from his mortal wound, seeking the dark of his lair like a wild animal that has its death-hurt. But he had not died alone as a wild animal dies. In the dreadful sea-cavern where they dwelt his mother had been waiting his return.

She was of the same kind as Grendel, monstrous, evil, a Death-Shadow-in-the-Dark; but she had possessed the power to love, and she had loved her son, and was therefore more terrible than he had ever been. Now, mad with grief as a bitch-wolf whose cubs are taken from her, panting for revenge, she followed the day-old blood-trail to the threshold of Heorot and hurled back the door.

Within was a sudden dreadful uproar. Men sprang from the sleeping benches, snatching up their weapons, but as no blade could bite on her son's charmed hide, so none could bite on hers. She surged forward, heedless of all that they could do against her, and with a triumphant yell she grasped Aschere, whom the King loved best of all his thanes, and next instant was gone with him into the night.

Lamentation swept through Heorot, where so short a time before had been laughter and the song of the harp. Word was carried to the King and he came and stood among them, with his grey beard wild from his pillow, and the tears of grief for Aschere his friend trickling down the deep-cut lines of his stern face.

Beowulf and his comrades, weary after their struggle of the night before, slept deep and dreamlessly, and heard no sound until Beowulf woke in the first greyness of the dawn, to find a hand shaking his shoulder and a voice crying in his ear that he must come to Hrothgar the King.

He flung a cloak round his nakedness and with his comrades went out after the messenger, and across the wet grass under the apple trees to Heorot the Hart. He found Hrothgar seated in his High Seat, no longer weeping but with his face as it were turned to stone.

'My lord Hrothgar, what has happened here in the night?'

The old man stared straight before him, and his voice was dull and hard. 'Evil has returned to Heorot.'

'What evil? Surely Grendel has not come again. What evil? Tell me!'

'Grendel? Nay, not Grendel. I have heard men speak before now of having seen not one but two Night-Stalkers among the moorland mists, and one of them in some sort like a woman. Fool that I was, and thrice-cursed fool. I paid no heed to the tale, but now I know all too surely that the tale was true. Dead is Aschere, my Councillor and shoulder-to-shoulder man. Many times we strove side by side in battle, shedding our blood together and sharing the mead horn afterwards; and now he is dead, slain by the foul kinswoman of the monster whom you slew.'

Beowulf straightened himself and shook off the last rags of sleep that still clung about him. 'I have still my strength, Hrothgar the King, and still it is at your service.'

Nothing changed in the stony face of the old King, only his hands clenched and unclenched on the carved foreposts of the Seat. 'Save us from this new horror, Beowulf, as you saved us from the other. You alone can do it. Yet not even you can bring back to life Aschere, who was near to me as my own heart.'

'Sorrow not so grievously,' Beowulf said quickly. 'It is better that a man should avenge his friend than mourn him overmuch. Each of us must wait the end of life, and if a man gain honour while he lives, as Aschere gained it, that is best for a warrior when the time comes that Wyrd cuts the web of his living from the loom. Abide but this one day and your friend shall not lie unavenged, though I cannot bring him back to you.' He covered the clenched hands with his own and looked into the stricken face of the King. 'Listen, and believe me. Not in Earth's breast nor in the fiery heart of the mountains nor the black depths of the sea shall the She-Wolf escape my coming.'

Hrothgar drew a long breath, and seemed to draw in strength with it as a gift from the young champion. Light came again into his eyes, and he got slowly to his full height and looked about him. 'Have my horse saddled, and others for Beowulf and whoever chooses to ride with us. We are for the Wolf-Woman's lair.'

Beowulf strode away to his own quarters, and even before the horses had been brought round, he had returned, wearing the ring-mail sark that was as fine as a salmon skin, and his own close-fitting helmet, and carrying his sword. And before the sun had risen clear of the rim of the hills he and Hrothgar, with a mingled company of Danes and Geats behind them, were pressing onward across the waste wet mosses of the moors, following Grendel's blood trail towards the sea-shore.

Far down the coast from the fjord with its

shingle strand where the Geatish war-galley lay behind her barricade of oars, was a very different place; a sea-inlet between two steep nesses, with a narrow opening to the sea outside. Along the base of the cliffs lay black shelving rocks where the sea beasts basked at noontide, and others that were jagged and fanged like sea beasts themselves, and the waves of the open sea, driven into the confined space, boiled and weltered as in a cauldron. At the landward end of this evil place a stream coming down from the high moors had cut for itself through the years a deep gorge overhung with a tangle of sere and salt-burned trees that dripped grey lichen into the grey mists of the falling water and the spume that beat up from the churning waves below. A place of ill-omen; a dreadful place of which men told many stories – stories of giant shapes half glimpsed in the sea mists, of strange sounds echoing and strange lights flaring beneath the water, and storms that blew up out of nowhere and strange tides that set there, while elsewhere along the coast the winds and the tides were fair. Land animals shunned the place, they said, and if a deer hard-pressed by the hounds were driven to the edge of the stream it would turn there on the bank and die, rather than plunge into the water and swim for safety.

To this place Grendel's blood trail led the

Geatish and Danish warriors, and on the cliff edge above it, lying abandoned like some fragment of a mouse that a great cat has dropped from its jaws, they found Aschere's head, where Grendel's Dam had torn it off before she plunged down to her lair.

Dismounting, the thanes gathered about it in silence. Hrothgar in their midst knelt stiffly beside the last dreadful relic of his dead sword-brother, and put back the tangle of blood-soaked hair with hands as gentle as a woman's; but he spoke no word – there was no word to speak. In a short while he rose, saying to the thanes about him, 'Hobble the horses; from here we must go on foot.'

One by one, following the old King and the young hero, they dropped over the edge out of the morning sunlight, and began the long climb down through the rocks and tree roots of the dark gorge to the foot of the cliffs. As they went, it seemed to every man that a cold murk, a shadow that was more than the headlands cutting off the light of day, rose about them, deadening heart and spirit; a shadow that grew chiller and more deadly with every downward step they took.

At last the gorge widened, the stream sprang out over a ledge and plunged down to join the churning waters of the sea-hole, and following it they came scrambling out from a world of trees into a world of spray-lashed rocks. On the rock ledges the great tusked seals and walruses lay basking, another menace to be outfaced; and all among the rocks the water was fouled with murky crimson as slow gouts of blood still came

welling up from below. The roar of the water
was in their ears, but under the roar, like the
still depths far down beneath the fret and turmoil of the surface waves, was a great silence.
No sea birds cried in this place, and the silence,
like the shadow, pressed upon the heart.

One of the Danes had brought a war-horn
with him, and in a gesture of defiance he put the
silver mouthpiece to his lips and set the dim
gorge and the gloom beneath the trees echoing
with the eager battle-music. The echoes flung
back and forth along the base of the cliffs,
splintering on the sheer rock faces, and the sea
beasts, roused from their sleep, plunged roaring
and bellowing into the water.

Beowulf snatched a bow from the Geat who
stood nearest to him. 'An arrow – quick, an
arrow, Scaef,' and when the other gave it to him
he notched it to the bowstring and drew and
loosed in one swift movement. The arrow sped
out into the midst of the threshing herd, and
stood quivering in the neck of a huge bull walrus.
The men with him set up a shout, and some
began to scramble out along the weed-slippery
rocks; a dozen spears and sharp walrus hooks
were in the body of the wildly struggling beast,
and it was dragged to land and killed with a
blow behind the head from a heavy shield rim.
For a few moments the Geats and Danes

gathered to stare and exclaim over it, for it was a great brute and would yield much ivory. But it was not for walrus hunting that they had come to this accursed place, and almost at once they turned away to the true venture in hand.

Beowulf had no preparations to make. He was already clad in his ring-mail sark, his boar-crested helm pulled low upon his brow, his sword in his hand – not the King's gift sword, but his own weapon that he had carried through many a fight by sea and land, and which fitted his grasp as if hand and hilt had been made for each other. But he was not, after all, to carry his own sword into the fight that was waiting for him, for at the last instant Hunferth the King's Jester, the bitter-tongued and flame-tempered, pulled the sword from his own wolfskin sheath and came shouldering through the other warriors to thrust it half angrily into Beowulf's hand. 'Here, take my sword – Hrunting, men call it. The blade was tempered with brew of poison twigs and hardened with battle blood. It is a powerful blade and has never yet failed its man in combat.'

Beowulf looked from the jester's face to the wave-grey blade in his hand, and slowly back again. This was the man who had flung insults in his teeth only two nights since. But he saw Hunferth regretted the insults now, and for him that was enough. He passed his own sword to the nearest of his Geats, and took the weapon which the other held out to him, smiling a little into the hot dark eyes. 'Friend, I thank you for the loan. With Hrunting, or surely not at all, I will overcome this Wolf-Woman of the sea.'

Then he turned to the King standing by. 'Hrothgar, Lord of the Danes, I go now, and whether we shall meet again is as Wyrd may choose. If I do not return, I pray you send those gifts which you gave to me home to Hygelac my own Hearth-Lord – all save the great sword; let you give that to Hunferth your Jester, as a gift from a friend in place of his sword Hrunting, which will have perished with me.'

For a long moment, the Jester's sword naked across his thighs, he stood looking about him, at the distant sunlight that he could see touching golden on the high crests of the headlands and the clear blue of the open sea beyond, wondering if ever he would feel the lifting deck of his war-boat beneath his feet again; looking into the troubled faces of one after another of his sword-brothers, and wondering if that also was for the last time.

'Wait for me here,' he said.

Then he turned from them all, and with the great sword held above his head, plunged down into the surf.

6. The Sea-Hag

Down and down sank Beowulf into the cold swinging depths; down and down for what seemed the whole of a day. From all sides the tusked sea beasts rushed in upon him, striving to gore him to pieces; and ever as he sank he fought them off with stroke and lunge of the great sword Hrunting. At last his feet touched the sea floor, and instantly an enemy far more dire was upon him, as the Sea-Hag leapt to fling her arms about him, clutching him to her with claws as terrible as her son's had been. He was being rushed through the black depths, close-locked in her dreadful embrace, and now, still together, they were diving upward through the under-water mouth of a cave.

Up and up ... They were in a vast sea-hall above the tide line, white sand underfoot, and the faint light of day falling in shafts from some opening to the clifftop far above. Beowulf tore himself free and springing clear for a sword stroke, brought Hrunting whistling down on her head. The cave rang with the blow, but for the first time since it was forged the blade refused

66

to bite, and next instant she was upon him once more. He stumbled beneath her onslaught and she flung him down with herself on top of him, stabbing again and again at his breast with her saex, her broad-bladed dagger, and when that failed to pierce his battle-sark clawing and worrying at him as though she were a wolf indeed. He saw her fangs sharp behind her snarling lips, and her eyes shone with balefire amid the tangle of her hair; but the ring-mail of the Queen's gift withstood her still, and gathering his strength he flung her off a second time, and springing up, aimed at her a blow that should have swept her head from her shoulders.

Again her charmed hide turned the stroke; and with a cry he flung the useless weapon aside. 'Come then, my naked hands shall serve me as they served me in the hall of Hrothgar!' and he sprang to meet her next attack.

There on the silver sand, with the roar of the sea echoing about them hollow like the echo in a vast shell, he with one arm locked about her and the other straining at her dagger wrist, she striving always with fang and claw to come at his heart, they reeled and trampled to and fro, as two nights since he had reeled and trampled to and fro with Grendel in the darkened hall of Heorot.

Long and bitter was the struggle, but there was a strength in the Sea-Hag that had not been in her son, and Beowulf could not overcome it. Some weapon he must have, and as he fought he snatched desperate glances about him in search of one. Here and there ancient weapons hung on the rock walls of the cavern, and among them the light from the roof fell upon one sword, a huge sword, dwarf-wrought perhaps for giants in the far-past days, for it was so long in the blade and broad in the grip that no mortal man save Beowulf could have wielded it. Seeing it,

his heart leapt up with fresh hope, and gathering all his strength and cunning he gave way before the Sea-Hag's onslaught, then swerved and sprang sideways past her, to snatch it from the wall. His hand closed over the hilt, and with a triumphant battle-shout he whirled around and brought the blade down upon her in a flashing swoop of fire.

It shored through hair and hide and bone, and Grendel's Dam dropped without a sound, her hideous head all but smitten from her shoulders.

Beowulf stood still, panting from his struggle, and looked about him, while the magic blade dripped red in his hand. Far off at the water's edge, the light from the upper world showed him the gigantic body of Grendel lying out-stretched, dead, and he strode towards it across the stained and trampled sand. Here at last, it seemed, he had a blade that could pierce the flesh of Grendel and his kin, and raising it once more with a mighty effort he smote loathsome head and loathsome body asunder. Blood streamed out into the water in a murky crimson flood that the sea sucked under and out through the mouth of the cave. And as Beowulf stood gazing down at the dead monster, the thick dark blood dripping along the blade ate into it and melted it away like ice in the warmth of a fire, until nothing was left but the wondrous gold-wrought hilt in his hand.

Then Beowulf stooped and twisted his free hand in the snaky hair of the severed head, and with the sword hilt still in the other, dived down to the cave mouth and triumphantly up through the water that was now clear and bright; up and up towards the daylight far above him.

Meanwhile the Geats and Danes had waited all the long-drawn day, watching from the deserted walrus rocks, and as the sun began to wester, they beheld a great gout of blood that came bursting up from the depths as though the sea-hole itself were vomiting blood. They crowded to the brink, staring downward with eyes that strained in their heads, but it was a sight to shake the boldest heart, and as the moments lengthened and brought no sign of Beowulf, the hope that they had clung to all day dwindled and grew thin like the red stain washing seaward on the waves.

At last Hrothgar stirred with a heavy sigh. 'It is over, then, and we shall not see him again, Beowulf who was as a son to me,' and he turned away to the rocky gloom under the trees where the stream came down. 'Come, there is nought to be gained by biding longer in this place.'

And sadly, like warriors straggling back from defeat, his thanes followed him as he set his face to the long upward climb.

But Beowulf's Geats remained, almost as empty of hope as those who followed Hrothgar, but faithful to their lord, who had bidden them wait for him. And hardly had the wave-roar engulfed the last sounds of the departing Danes, than Waegmund sprang up, pointing. 'Look! Look! The creatures are all making out to sea! It is as though they fled for their lives!' And another of the little band took up his cry. 'Look! Look at the water! It is clean and clear!' and as they slithered and stumbled forward to the outermost edges of the weed-slippery rocks, shouting to each other while the great walruses swam away, they saw far down through the water that was clear now as green crystal, the longed-for shape of Beowulf springing up towards them.

Eager arms reached down to aid him ashore as he broke surface, scattering the white foam from his shoulders; and then he was among them, stretched, spent, upon the rocks, drawing the free air into himself in great gasps like a runner at the end of a hard-won race, while they thronged about him to loosen off his helmet and stare with awe and wonder at the blind snarling head that he had flung down beside him, and the huge bladeless sword hilt he still clutched in his hand.

'Oh, it is good to see your faces again, my brothers!' said Beowulf as soon as he could speak; and then looking about him, 'But where are Hrothgar and his thanes? Did they find the waiting over-long?'

'They saw the wave of blood that boiled up from below,' said Waegmund, kneeling beside

him, 'and their hearts told them that there was nothing more to wait for.'

'That was the blood of the Sea-Hag, and Grendel's blood that gushed out when I smote his head from his body lying dead down there,' Beowulf said. 'And you? Did you not also see the blood-wave?'

'Aye, we saw it.'

'But your hearts did not bid you lose hope?'

Waegmund bent his head. 'As to hope, there was little enough of that left to us, but we were still your war-boat's crew, your shoulder-to-shoulder men.'

'And so you stayed,' Beowulf said. And suddenly he laughed on a note that was like the song of victorious war-horns, and sprang up, holding out his arms to them. 'And that is well, for see, it will take four spears at the least to carry the monster's head back to Heorot!'

And so, with Grendel's head upreared on four spear points in their midst, they turned to the gorge that led up towards the high moors, and leaving the sea-hole cleansed of evil behind them, set out on their triumphant way back to the settlement.

7. The Sail-Road Home

The sun was sinking fast as they came down through the tilled land to Heorot, and their shadows stretched out sideways far across the young barley, and high on the gable end of the King's hall the gilded antlers of the stag caught the last of the sunset and flared like a branch of many-forked flames. Folk came running to house-place doorways as they passed, but the champions strode straight on to the King's threshold and up through the hall, to fling the grizzly head down at Hrothgar's feet where he sat sorrowfully in his High Seat.

'Rouse up and be glad, Hrothgar of the Danes!' Beowulf cried. 'Look now upon the sea-spoil that we bring you.'

But Hrothgar, leaning forward in his chair, was already looking, as though there was nothing else in all the world to look at but Grendel's severed head lying among the rushes at his feet. Then he raised his own head and looked at Beowulf and the triumphant Geats behind him.

'I never thought to see you stand again in this

hall, Beowulf son of Ecgtheow,' he said slowly, and then, 'The Dam also is dead?'

'The Dam also is dead, but I could bring you only this one head for a trophy. One head, and the sword with which I smote it off. But see, only the hilt is left; the blood of the monster melted the blade away,' and Beowulf held out to the King the huge sword hilt that was wrought all over with writhing golden serpents.

Hrothgar took and gazed at it in wonder. Then looking up again, he said, 'So, there has been a great fight and many marvels here. Tell me now the story of all that has passed since you dived into the waves above the Night-Stalker's lair.'

And so, standing proudly before the old King as he sat with the ancient hilt in his hands, Beowulf told of his fight with the Sea-Hag, making of the story a kind of triumph song as he went along, after the way of his people when there was a victory to relate.

When the song was ended, Hrothgar rose from his seat and flung his arms about the young champion's shoulders, and could find no words to speak, because Aschere was worthily avenged and henceforth men might indeed sleep safely in Heorot the Hart.

That night the Geats and Danes feasted together as they had feasted the night before, and more gifts were showered upon Beowulf and his

77

sword-brothers, and the mead horns passed round and the fires leapt high, and the King's bard woke the music of his harp. And when it grew late and the time for mead and harp-song was past, Geats and Danes together slept peacefully in Heorot until the first light stole across the moors and the cocks were crowing.

When the sun was up and the settlement busy about the new day, Beowulf sought out the King

in his own place. 'The thing that we came to do is done,' he said. 'Heorot is a safe sleeping place henceforth; and now it is time that I go back to Hygelac, my own King and House-Lord.'

'My heart is sore to lose you,' said Hrothgar. 'But you must go back to your own House-Lord and your own people,' and he rose from among the wolfskins of the bench where he was sitting, and held Beowulf at arms' length and looked deep into his face. 'I think that in the long years ahead, you will be such a sword and such a shield to your people as they may well have need of.'

'That is as Wyrd decrees,' said Beowulf, and he set his hands over the old man's on his shoulders. 'But this I know, that you have called me your son, and if ever you should need me, whether it be under threat of war or for any other cause, you have but to send me word, and I will come with a thousand warriors at my back.'

And Hrothgar bowed his head on to Beowulf's shoulder and wept and they vowed friendship for all time between Geats and Danes, and spat and struck their palms together as men sealing a bargain.

Then Beowulf called his companions together, and they took their leave and set out once more along the paved road to the coast, some riding the horses that Hrothgar had given to their leader, some walking, all laden with treasures of gold and fine weapons, and their grey ring-mail sounding on them as they moved.

It was still early when, with a great company of Danes still about them, they came over the moorland ridge and down to the head of the fjord where their war-boat lay secure on the shingle above the tide mark, and the Coast Warden, sitting his horse beside her, looked as though he had never been away. To him Beowulf gave a sword with gold wires about the hilt, brother to one which he had given Hunferth; and then with the Danes to help them, they set rollers under the keel and, shouting and cheering, ran their boat down into the surf, feeling her grow light and buoyant and wake to life again as the lift of the water took her. They got the horses aboard and bestowed them with the rest of the treasure in the hollow heart of the ship below the mast, and springing aboard themselves they hung their round linden shields along the bulwarks and ran out the oars. And with Beowulf leaning to the steering-oar they brought her round and set her eager dragon-head seaward. The farewell shouts of the Danes grew fainter astern until their voices were lost in the crying of the gulls; and presently as they cleared the high nesses at the fjord mouth the open sea was before them and the wind came to fill their striped sail and speed them on their wave-road home.

Two days later, Hygelac's Coast Warden, sitting his horse high on the cliffs of Geatland, saw, as Hrothgar's Coast Warden had seen, a long war-boat running in to land. But this was no strange vessel, and he was watching for her already. At sight of her a shout of joy burst from him, and driving his heel again and again into his horse's flank, he urged it at a gallop down towards the keel-strand below Hygelac's Hall, crying out the news to all he passed on the way.

So when Beowulf and his sword companions ran their keel ashore, they found a glad throng of their own folk waiting on the tide line to greet them and give them their aid as they set their shoulders to the sides of the vessel and ran her far up the shelving strand, and help them to carry the treasure up to Hygelac's Hall.

That night there was feasting and rejoicing in the royal Hall of Geatland, and Hygd the Queen poured the mead for the returned champions, and Beowulf, when they shouted for him to tell the tale of all that had passed since he sailed for Denmark, rose in his place and flinging back his head, made his triumph song of the slaying of Grendel and the slaying of Grendel's Dam. And when the story was done, he called for the treasures that he had won to be brought out, and gave away to the King his House-Lord, and to the Queen and to his friends and kinsfolk everything save Hrothgar's first gift-sword and the horse with Hrothgar's saddle on it, which he kept for himself.

Then, as a man takes up a well-worn and familiar garment, he resumed again his accustomed place as chief among the warriors and champions of Hygelac.

8. The Fire-Drake's Hoard

The years went by and the years went by, bringing as they passed great changes to the two kingdoms. In Denmark Hrothgar died and was howe-laid, and Hrethric his son ruled in his place. Hygelac fell in an expedition against the Frisians, and Beowulf, still his chief thane, avenged him worthily on the enemy and then, sore wounded himself, fought his way back to the seashore and the waiting war-galleys, and so escaped to carry the sad tidings back to Hygd the Queen. Heardred the King's son was still only a boy, too young to lead his people in war or guide them wisely in peace, and so the Queen called together the Councillors and foremost chieftains of the land, and with their consent offered the gold collar of the Kingship to Beowulf in his stead. But Beowulf, true to his House-Lord, would have nothing to say to this, and so Heardred, young as he was, was raised to the High Seat with his mighty cousin to stand ever at his side as counsellor and protector.

Alas! It was all to no avail, for in his young manhood Heardred fell in battle as his father had done. And this time, when the Kingship was offered to him again Beowulf took it, though with a heavy heart, for he was the rightful next of kin.

Long and gloriously he ruled, holding his people strongly and surely as in the hollow of his great sword hand. Fifty times the wild geese flew south in the autumn, fifty times the birch buds quickened in the spring and the young men ran the war-keels down from the sheds; and in all that time Geatland prospered as never before. But when the fiftieth year was over, a terror fell upon the land.

And this was the way of it.

Many hundreds of years before, a family of mighty warriors had gathered by inheritance and by strength in war an immense store of treasure, gold cups and crested helmets, arm-rings of earls and necklaces of queens, ancient swords and armour wrought with magic spells by the dwarf-kind long ago. A great war of many battles had carried away all this kinsfolk save one, and he, lonely and brooding on the fate of the precious things that he and his kin had gathered with such joy when he also should have gone by the Dark Road, made ready a secret fastness that he knew of, a cave under the headland that men called the Whale's Ness. And there, little by little, he carried all his treasures and hid them within sounding of the sea, and made a death-song over them as over slain warriors, lamenting for the thanes who would drink from the golden cups and wield the mighty swords no more, for the hearths grown cold and the harps fallen silent and the halls abandoned to the foxes and the ravens.

When the man died the hoard was forgotten and lay unknown under the flank of the hill while the slow centuries went by, until at last a fire-dragon, seeking a lair among the rocks, came upon the hidden entrance to the cave and, crawling within, found the treasure. Because he had found it the fire-drake thought that it was his, and he loved it, heavy arm-ring and jewelled dagger and gold-wrought cup; and he flung his slithering coils about it, and lay brooding over it for three hundred years.

But at the end of that time a man who had angered his chieftain in some way and was fleeing from his wrath also found the hidden entrance among the rocks, and the golden hoard, and the dragon sleeping.

Now through all those three hundred years the dragon had been slowly growing, until from snout to tail tip he was ten times as long as a man is tall. Yet still he was not long enough completely to encircle the mound of treasure, and between snout and tail tip as he

lay was a gap just wide enough to let through a man.

The fugitive saw the golden glimmer of the hoard, and even while his brain swam at the sight it seemed to him that here might be a way out of his desperate plight. Creeping between snout and tail tip of the sleeping dragon, he caught up a golden cup, one great cup glowing like the sun with which to buy off his chieftain's wrath, and, clutching it to his breast, fled back the way he had come.

Presently the fire-drake woke, and knew in the moment of his waking that he had been robbed. Blindly, in grief and fury, he snuffed about his beloved hoard, and knew by the smell that a man had been there. He crawled outside and padded about the entrance to the cave and among the rocks, and found man's footprints; and when the dusk came down he spread his great wings and flew out in search of the thief.

Night after night from that time forward he flew out, filled with hatred, and seeking not only the thief but to wreak his vengeance on all men because it was a man who had robbed him. Far and wide he flew, from coast to coast of Geatland, wrapped in his own fiery breath as though in mists of flame. Houses, men, trees and cattle, even the King's Hall itself, shrivelled up as his angry breath blew upon them, and at each sunrise when he returned to his lair, he left the trail of his night's flying marked in black and smoking desolation across the land.

Beowulf was old now, a grey warrior who had once been golden, but a warrior still. Also he was the King; and for him in the last resort was the duty and the privilege of dying for the life of his people. And so, as he had done so many times before, he made himself ready for battle. Well he knew that he would not be able to come to grips with the dragon as he had done in his youth with Grendel the Night-Stalker, for now he had to fight not only strength but fire, and his familiar war-gear would not serve him, for how long could a shield of linden-wood withstand flame? So he sent for the Warsmith to come to him in his sleeping quarters – now that his hall was no more than a blackened shell – and said to him, 'Forge me a shield of iron, strong to withstand fire. And be quick in the forging of it, for the people cannot endure many more such nights of desolation.' And he chose twelve thanes of his own bodyguard, among them Wiglaf, grandson of that Waegmund who had sailed with him for Denmark fifty roving-seasons ago, and bade them make ready to accompany him.

There was a thirteenth of their company also, for the chieftain for whom the cup had been stolen had handed over the thief to Beowulf when he saw the evil that the theft had caused; and to him Beowulf said, quietly terrible, 'You and you alone of all living men know in what place the Terror-that-flies-by-Night has his lair; and if you lead us to the spot, it may be that you shall continue among living men. Your chances shall be no better and no worse than those of my companions who come with me. But if you fail to lead us truly to the place, then you may escape the fire-drake, but assuredly *you shall not escape me*!'

So next morning the King put on his grey ring-mail sark, and sheathed at his side the ancient sword that had been his companion in every fight since Hrothgar gave it to him. And he took the heavy iron shield that was still warm from the anvil, and bidding the rest of his war-host to follow on behind he rode out with his twelve chosen thanes on his last adventure.

The cave below the Whale's Ness was more than two days' ride from the royal village, but they pressed on with desperate speed, by dark as well as by day, and on the next morning, having left the weary horses behind them among the trees, they came over a wooded ridge and found themselves looking down upon what must once have been a fair and pleasant valley, dipping to low sea-cliffs at one end and at the other running up to meet the high moors where the bees droned among the heather bloom. It was blackened and desolate now, a landscape of despair, fanged with the stumps of charred tree trunks. On the far side of the valley the blunt turf slope of the Ness upheaved itself and thrust its great head out to sea. And against the flank of the Whale's Ness the ground was tumbled and broken up into low cliffs and rocky outcrops over which a faint smoke hung.

The thief halted on the edge of the trees and pointed, trembling. 'There, down there where the smoke curls among the rocks; that is where the fire-drake has his lair and guards his treasure. I have brought you to the place as you bade me, and there is no further use that you can have for such as I am. Now be merciful as you are mighty, my lord Beowulf, and let me go.'

Beowulf glanced at him in scorn. 'Even as you say, I have no further use for such as you. Go where you will, then; your part is done.' And when the man had scurried back into the woods, he seated himself on a fallen tree bole, to rest and gather strength, his elbows on his knees, his gaze going down into the valley and across it to the tumble of rocks under the green flank of the Whale's Ness. And sitting there he felt Wyrd touch him, like a shadow passing across the sun. He had been young and confident, glorying in his own strength when he fought his battle with

Grendel, but now he was old and he knew that this would be his last fight. And suddenly lifting his head he began as the wild swans are said to do to sing his own death-song. 'I have lived a long life, and all since before I was seven summers old, I remember.' He sang of his contest with Breca son of Beanstan, and of Hygelac his House-Lord, and the companions who had been his war-boat's crew and sailed with him for Denmark, and the fights with Grendel and his Dam. He sang of the death of Hygelac and the death of Heardred, and his own coming to the Kingship. 'The Frankish warrior who slew Hygelac my King, him I slew with my naked hands, even as I slew Grendel the Night-Stalker,' and with the words, he sighed, and it seemed that all at once he had come to the end of his song. 'But this fight that waits for me now is a different thing, and I am old. Yet the battle-power is not yet fallen away from me, and I am still the King.' He looked about him at the warriors gathered on the woodshore, and slowly got to his feet, holding out his hand for the great iron shield.

Wiglaf gave it to him, stammering in desperate eagerness, 'My King and House-Lord – I beg you let me come with you!'

Beowulf shook his head, but his eyes were kindly as he looked at the young warrior. 'Na, na, did I not say that I am the King? This is a fight, not for a war-host but for one man, even as my fight with Grendel was for one man. But stay here, all of you, with your weapons ready, and watch to see how it goes with me down yonder.'

And he took up the heavy shield and walked out from among them, out from among the charred trees and down into the valley of desolation, his sword naked in his hands.

9. The Death of Beowulf

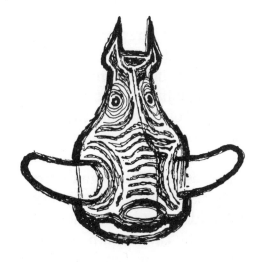

As Beowulf drew near to the gigantic rock-tumble under the Whale's Ness, he saw in the midst of it the dark mouth of a cave about which the smoke hung more thickly than elsewhere. A stream broke out from the darkness of it, flowing away down the slope of the valley, the water boiling as it came, and flickered over with the vaporous flame of dragon's breath; and Beowulf, with his shield before his face, forced his way up beside it until he reached the trampled ground before the cave mouth and could go no further for the choking fumes and smoke that poured out from the darkness under the flank of the hill.

There he stood, and beat sword upon shield and shouted his defiance to the fire-drake within. His shout rose like a storm, the war-cry that his thanes had heard above the clamour of many and many a battlefield; it pierced in through the opening among the rocks, and the fire-drake heard it and awoke. A great cloud of fiery breath belched out from the cave mouth, and within there sounded the clapping of mighty wings; and even as the King flung up his shield to guard his face, the earth shook and roared and the dragon came coiling from its lair.

Heat played over its scales so that they changed colour, green and blue and gold, as the colours play on a sword-blade heated for tempering, and all the air danced and quivered about him. Fire was in his wings and a blasting flame leapt from his eyes. With wings spread, he half-flew half-sprang at Beowulf, who stood firm to meet him and swung up his sword for a mighty blow. The bright blade flashed down, wounding the monster in the head: but though the skin gaped and the stinking blood sprang forth, the bones of the skull turned the blow so that the wound was not mortal. Bellowing, the creature crouched back, then sprang again, and Beowulf was wrapped from head to heel in a cloud of fire. The iron rings of his mail seared him to the bone and the great shield of smith's work glowed red-hot as he strove to guard his face and bring up his blade for another blow.

On the hill above the watching thanes saw the terrible figure of their lord in its rolling shroud of flame, and brave men though they had been in battle, terror seized them and they turned to fly; all save one. Wiglaf, grandson of Waegmund, and the youngest of them all, stood firm. For one despairing moment he tried to rally the rest, crying after them to remember their loyalty to their House-Lord. 'Brave things we promised in the King's hall when we drank his mead and took the gifts he gave us! Often we swore ourselves his men to the death – and now the death comes, we forget! Shame to us for ever if we bear home our shields in safety from this day; but I will not share the shame!' And snatching up his shield and dragging his sword from its sheath, he began to run also, not back towards the safety of the woods, but forward and down into the smoke-filled valley.

Head down and shield up, he plunged into the fiery reek, shouting, 'Beowulf, beloved lord, I come! Remember the battles of your youth and stand strong – I am here beside you!'

Beowulf heard his young kinsman's voice and felt him at his shoulder, yellow linden shield beside that of glowing iron, and his heart took new strength within him. But the sound of another voice roused the dragon to yet greater hatred, and the earth groaned and the rocks shivered to his fury, while he drove out blast on blast of searing flame. Wiglaf's shield blackened and flamed like a torch, and he flung the blazing remnant from him and sprang to obey his lord as Beowulf shouted to him, 'Here! Behind my targe – it shall serve to cover us both!' And steady and undismayed they fought on behind the red-hot shield of iron.

But at last, as it came whistling down in mighty blow, Beowulf's sword that had seen the victory in a hundred battles shivered into fragments on the dragon's head.

With a great cry, the King threw the useless hilt away from him, but before he could snatch the saex from his belt, the fire-drake was upon him, rearing up under the flailing darkness of its wings, the poisonous foreclaws slashing at his throat above the golden collar.

In the same instant, while the King's life blood burst out in a red wave, Wiglaf sprang clear of the iron targe and, diving low under the fire-drake, stabbed upward with shortened blade into its scaleless underparts.

A convulsive shudder ran through all the lashing coils of the dragon's body, and instantly the fire began to fade, and as it faded, Beowulf with the last of his battle strength, tore the saex from his belt and hurling himself forward, hacked the great brute almost in two.

The dragon lay dead, with the brightness of its fires darkening upon it. But Beowulf also had got his death hurt, and now as he stood swaying above the huge carcass, his wounds began to burn and swell, the venom from the monster's talons boiled in his breast and all his limbs seemed on fire. Blindly he staggered towards a place where the rocks made a natural

couch close beside the cave entrance, and sank down upon it, gasping for air.

Wiglaf with his own burns raw upon him bent over his lord, loosened the thongs of his helmet and lifted it away so that the cool sea wind was on his forehead; brought water in his own helmet from the stream, which now ran cool and clear, to bathe Beowulf's face and wounds, all the while calling to him, calling him back from somewhere a long way off. By and by Beowulf's head cleared a little, and for a while the scalding tide of poison seemed to ebb, and the old King gathered up strength to speak, knowing that his time for speaking would soon be done. 'Now I wish in my heart that the All-Father had granted me a son to take my war-harness after me; but since that may not be, you must be son to me in this, and take my helm and good saex, and my battle-sark from my body after I am dead, and wear them worthily for my sake.'

He felt Wiglaf's tears upon his face and gathered himself again. 'Na, na, here is no cause for weeping. I am an old man and have lived my life and fought my battles. Fifty winters I have held rule over my people and made them strong so that never a war-host dared to cross our frontiers. I have not sought out feuds, nor sworn many oaths and lightly broken them; and when my life goes out from my body I shall not have to answer to the All-Father for slain kinsfolk or unjust rule.'

He propped himself on to his elbow and looked about him, and his gaze came to rest on the carcass of the fire-drake lying sprawled before the entrance to the cave. 'I have paid away my life to slay the thing which would have slain my people, and now I see it lying dead before me. But if the thief's tale be true, then I have won for them in my last battle some store of treasure also, and that too I would see before the light goes from my eyes. Go now, Wiglaf, my kinsman, and bring out to me what you can carry.'

Wiglaf, who had been kneeling at his lord's side, got to his feet and stumbling past the still twitching coils of the dead monster, went into the cave.

Within the entrance he came to a halt, staring with scarce-believing eyes at the piled-up wonders of the fire-drake's hoard. Golden cups and pitchers, jewelled collars for a king's throat, ancient ring-mail and boar-masked helmets and swords eaten through with rust; and upreared high above the rest, a golden banner curiously wrought with long-forgotten magic, which shone of itself, and shed about it a faint light in which he saw all the rest. But he had neither the time nor the heart for much marvelling. In frantic haste he loaded himself with cups and arm-rings and weapons, and the banner last of all, and carried them out into the daylight and flung them clanging down at the old man's feet.

Beowulf lay still with his eyes closed, and the blood still flowing from his wounds. But when Wiglaf fetched more water from the stream and again bathed his face he revived once more, and opened his eyes to gaze upon the treasure as it lay glittering among the rocks. 'A fine bright gleam of gold to light me on my way,' he said. 'Glad am I that since the time has come for me to go I may leave behind me such treasure for my people.' Then his gaze abandoned the glitter of the dragon's hoard, and went out and upward to where the great bluff forehead of the Whale's Ness upreared itself against the sky. 'After the bale-fire is burned out, bid them raise me a burial howe on the Whale's Ness yonder, a tall howe on the cliff edge, that it may serve as a mark for seafaring men such as I was in my youth. So they may see it from afar as they pass on the Sail-Road, and say, "There stands Beo-wulf's Barrow" and remember me.'

For the last time his gaze went to young Wig-laf's face, and his hands were at his wounded throat, fumbling off the golden collar of the Kingship. 'Take this also, with my war-gear.'

His voice was only a whisper now. 'Use it well, for you are the last of our kindred. One by one, Wyrd has swept them all away at their fated hour; and now it is time for me to go to them.'

And with the words scarce spoken, a great sigh broke from him and he fell back into the young warrior's arms. And Wiglaf laid him down.

He was still sitting at his dead lord's shoulder when a shadow fell across them both and, looking up slowly, he saw that the King's Hearth Companions had come stealing down from the high woods of their refuge, and were standing about him staring down in shame at slain hero and slain monster. He did not trouble to rise, but sitting drearily where he was, stony-eyed, he flayed them with all the bitter scorn that was in his heart. 'So you come, do you, now that the fire is spent! Well may men say, seeing you safe and unmarked in the war-gear that Beowulf gave you, that he made a bad bargain with his gifts. When his sorest need came upon him he had no cause to boast of his companions in arms. Small honour will Geatland have in her foremost warriors, when the princes of other lands hear of this day's work! Aye, you have kept whole your skins under your bright battle-sarks; but it may be that death is better for a warrior than a life of shame!'

And the thanes stood silent about their dead lord, enduring the lash of Wiglaf's scorn, for there was nothing that they could say.

Presently a scout sent out by the following war-host came riding over the wooded ridge and looked down into the valley. One long look was enough, and then wheeling his horse he galloped back to tell what he had seen. 'The fight is over, and our King lies dead among the rocks with the fire-drake dead beside him. Now the joy and honour that he gave us are fled from the land, and the War Chieftains will come against us as they have not dared to do for fifty years, and Beowulf who should have led us against them is dead.'

A groan ran through the host at his words, and at an increased pace they pressed on towards the dragon's lair.

When they came down into the blackened valley they found all as the messenger had told them, the grey-headed King lying dead with his broken sword beside him, and the carcass of the fire-drake outstretched on the burned and blood-soaked turf nearby; the shamed thanes standing at a distance, and Wiglaf sitting bowed with grief at his lord's shoulder; the golden gleam of the dragon's hoard among the rocks and, upreared over all, the great gold-wrought banner curving to the sea wind like the curved sail of a ship.

Sadly the warriors gathered about their King, and then at last Wiglaf stirred and rose to his feet, stiffly as though he too were an old man. He took up the golden collar of the Kingship, stained as it was with the dead hero's blood, and standing there before the sorrowing war-host he fastened it about his own neck. And with it he put on the King's authority. 'Beowulf is dead, and plainly you may see how he met his end. Gladly he paid away his life to save his people from the Terror-that-flew-by-Night, and in his dying he bade me greet you and pray you, after the bale-fire is burned out, to build him a worthy barrow for his resting-place – a great barrow high on the Whale's Ness, to be a guiding-mark hereafter for all who sail the sea. Now make ready the funeral pyre, and bring something to serve as a bier, that we may carry our old King to his chosen place. And meanwhile let seven of you come with me into the cave and bring out into the daylight all that yet remains there of the fire-drake's hoard.'

So while Wiglaf and the seven toiled to and fro, bringing out from the dark the treasure that had not seen the sun for a thousand years, others set themselves to gather wood and build a pyre high on the Whale's Ness and hand it round with war helms and fine weapons and ring-mail sarks, as befitted a King's funeral pyre. And yet others dragged the carcass of the fire-drake to the cliff's edge and heaved it over into the surf that creamed below. They brought a farm wain drawn by oxen and hung it round with shields as though its sides were the bulwarks of a war-boat, and when all was ready they laid the dead King in it, and piled about him the wrought gold and wondrous weapons of the dragon's hoard – for Wiglaf said, 'As Beowulf alone won all these things, so let them go back with him into the dark from which they came,' and in all the war-host no man lifted a voice against him.

Then they set the four slow yoke of oxen straining up the steep slope to the headland, where the pyre stood waiting against the sky. They laid the body of Beowulf on the stacked brushwood and thrust in the torches, and presently all men far and wide saw the red fire on the Whale's Ness, and knew that Beowulf had gone to join his kindred.

All night long the fire burned, and when it sank at dawn they piled about the ashes the precious things of the dragon's hoard, and up-reared the golden banner over all. Then they set themselves to raise the barrow as the old King had bidden them. For ten days they laboured, building it high and strong for the love that they had borne him, and on the tenth day the great howe of piled stones stood finished, notching the sky for all time on the uttermost height of the Whale's Ness, where the cliffs plunged sheer to the sea.

Then twelve chieftains of his bodyguard rode sunwise about it, singing the death song that the harpers had made for him. And when the song was sung, all men went away, and left Beowulf's barrow alone with the sea wind and the wheeling gulls and the distant ships that passed on the Sail-Road.

M Books is a new series consisting of some of the best contemporary fiction for young people.

Other books you may enjoy are:

The Day of the Pigeons Roy Brown
The Eighteenth Emergency Betsy Byars
The Pinballs Betsy Byars
After the Goat Man Betsy Byars
Time Trap Nicholas Fisk
The Slave Dancer Paula Fox
Black Jack Leon Garfield
My Side of the Mountain Jean George
I Am David Anne Holm
Fish Alison Morgan
The Cats Joan Phipson
Horned Helmet Henry Treece
The Crane Reiner Zimnik

The Eighteenth Emergency Betsy Byars
Benjamin Fawley knows why everyone at school calls him
Mouse, and he has never felt as scared as when he hears the
words 'Hammerman is after Mouse'. For Hammerman is the
school bully and Mouse has made a joke about him. Though
Mouse's friend Ezzie has the answer to life's seventeen greatest
emergencies he does not have the answer to the eighteenth: a
bully on the warpath. No one knows the answer to that.
Mouse will have to face Hammerman....
ISBN 0 333 24082 0

The Crane Reiner Zimnik
The town council builds the tallest crane in the world and puts
it in the charge of a young man with a blue feather in his cap.
He climbs to the driver's cabin at the top and stays there.
From his perch he watches the town change, a circus come
and go, a war come and go, a flood sweep in to cover the
land. Then he is alone, except for his friend the eagle. But he
keeps the crane in working order until a new world grows up
beneath him. And then it is time to move on.
ISBN 0 333 24486 9

I Am David Anne Holm
David has known no other life than that of the concentration
camp. Then he is allowed to escape. Reserved and watchful,
he wanders through Europe, fearful that *They* will catch him,
mistrustful of everyone he meets. This world outside the camp
is so strange to him he does not even know what things are
good to eat and what bad. Only gradually on his long and
dangerous journey does he lose his fear and mistrust and learn
why he was allowed to escape.
ISBN 0 333 24487 7

After the Goat Man Betsy Byars
Harold and Ada were playing Monopoly on Ada's porch when
they first met the strange, skinny boy called Figgy. And then
they discovered that Figgy's grandfather was none other than
the notorious 'Goat Man' whose picture had been in all the
papers and whose name had been mentioned on the radio
news that very day.

The Goat Man had fought a battle to prevent a new interstate highway being built across the land where he lived with Figgy in an old wooden cabin. Though, in the end, he had allowed the authorities to move him and Figgy into a modern house, he had changed his mind. And now... today... the Goat Man was barricaded into his cabin with a shotgun. Figgy had to do something. And Harold and Ada decided they couldn't let Figgy save the old man on his own. They would have to help. It was a problem that brought about some unexpected results.
ISBN 0 333 27861 5

Fish Alison Morgan
Fish is what they called Jimmy Barnes when he came to live in a small Welsh village. There was already a Jimmy living there, and when Jimmy Barnes boasted he was good at swimming, the others decided to call him Fish.

The two Jimmys were on their way home one day when they found a stray dog. Fish at once decided to keep it for his own. "I'm going to tell my dad she was found straying and Mr Thomas asked me to look after her till they found a proper owner."

It was a lie that was the start of a hard fight Fish had to keep his dog, and that led in the end to his fighting to save its life. For that night some sheep were killed by a dog on Jimmy Price's farm...

This is the story of a boy trying to prove himself and to find friendship despite the odds set against him.
ISBN 0 333 27865 8

The Cats Joan Phipson
When his family won top prize in the lottery, Jim couldn't help telling everyone. The good times were coming. But then Jim and his brother Willy took a lift from Kevin and Socker, only to find they were being kidnapped. Socker wanted the lottery money, and took the brothers into hiding in the wild Australian bush country.

What Socker and Kevin had not counted on was Willy's strange power and an unexpected enemy that lurked in the mists...
ISBN 0 333 27866 6

The Day of the Pigeons Roy Brown

Mousy Lawson runs away from Approved School one Friday evening. He is determined to find his father who has just written saying he has married again and is leaving the country after completing a little business. Mousy gets a lift in a lorry, reaches London, finds an empty basement in which to live, and starts looking for his father. That's when Chris enters Mousy's life, in search of Monsieur Poirot's prize pigeons. Unwillingly Chris is dragged into Mousy's search and before long he is not sure what to do about Mousy – or Mousy's criminal father.

ISBN 0 333 25715 4

I Am David Anne Holm

David has known no other life than that of the concentration camp. Then he is allowed to escape. Reserved and watchful, he wanders through Europe, fearful that *They* will catch him, mistrustful of everyone he meets. This world outside the camp is so strange to him he does not even know what things are good to eat and what bad. Only gradually on his long and dangerous journey does he lose his fear and mistrust and learn why he was allowed to escape.

ISBN 0 333 24487 7

Time Trap Nicholas Fisk

The year is 2079. Most of the earth is a poisoned wasteland. People live in Homebody Units and spend their time watching the Viddy screen. But Dano rebels against this mindless existence. He is befriended by the eccentric Uncle Lipton, a failed galactic pilot, who is more than 130 years old and still going strong, thanks to the secret life-prolonging drug Xtend, which also enables him to travel in time. Thinking he can escape the present, Dano agrees to travel with Uncle Lipton. But the drug's time-travel effects are only temporary. At the moment he sees his own terrifying future, he realises the drug cannot help him.

ISBN 0 333 24318 8

Published by Macmillan Education